Pay Less When Shopping

How to Take Full Advantage of Coupon Codes

By: Helen Anderson

9781635014259

I0510814

PUBLISHERS NOTES

Disclaimer – Speedy Publishing LLC

This publication is intended to provide helpful and informative material. It is not intended to diagnose, treat, cure, or prevent any health problem or condition, nor is intended to replace the advice of a physician. No action should be taken solely on the contents of this book. Always consult your physician or qualified health-care professional on any matters regarding your health and before adopting any suggestions in this book or drawing inferences from it.

The author and publisher specifically disclaim all responsibility for any liability, loss or risk, personal or otherwise, which is incurred as a consequence, directly or indirectly, from the use or application of any contents of this book.

Any and all product names referenced within this book are the trademarks of their respective owners. None of these owners have sponsored, authorized, endorsed, or approved this book.

Always read all information provided by the manufacturers' product labels before using their products. The author and publisher are not responsible for claims made by manufacturers.

This book was originally printed before 2014. This is an adapted reprint by Speedy Publishing LLC with newly updated content designed to help readers with much more accurate and timely information and data.

Speedy Publishing LLC

40 E Main Street, Newark, Delaware, 19711

Contact Us: 1-888-248-4521

Website: http://www.speedypublishing.co

REPRINTED Paperback Edition: 9781635014259:

Manufactured in the United States of America

DEDICATION

This book is dedicated to my number one fan, my Grandma Tessa.

TABLE OF CONTENTS

CHAPTER 1- INCREASING SALES AND CUSTOMER LOYALTY WITH COUPON CODES

Coupons can be used in just about every business. I've sat and thought and thought about it, but I can't think of any business that coupons can't be used in.

Coupons can be used to drive traffic to your site, reach new customers, entice past customers to purchase from you again, to sell big ticket items by offering a discount on them, to get customers to buy more from you, and so many other different ways.

Coupons can also create a "buzz" about your business. There are people who specialize in what is called "buzz marketing". I'm sure you've buzzed about a product. Have you ever bought a product and been so delighted with it that you told your family and friends, or even complete strangers that were standing in the grocery isle next to you thinking about buying this product. Then you have "buzzed". That's exactly what coupons can do for your business.

If you are offering a coupon for your product or service, and you get one happy customer you can bet they are going to tell others. This will set off a viral buzz that will bring more and more people to your business. Are you starting to see how these coupons can be used in several different ways to create more income and/or prospects? Well then keep reading because I've got a lot more information about this super marketing tactic that's really going to get you excited.

Now, I want you to take out a sheet of paper or open up your word processor and think of the products or services in your business that you could offer a discount on.

Here's what my list looks like:

I could:

1. Offer a discount on my consulting services.

2. Offer a buy one get one free offer on advertising services I offer.

3. Offer a coupon for free stuff when someone joins one of my membership sites.

4. Offer a $X discount on my eBooks, and software.

I know your business may be different than mine, but you can still find at least one thing to offer a discount on or a free offer for buying what you are selling. If you can't think of anything, compile a list of everything your business offers, then go back over that list, and I am sure you will find something. If you STILL can't find something, then my advice would be to develop or buy something inexpensive that you can either give away free or offer a discount on to achieve the goal you have for using coupons.

We'll talk about why and how to use coupons in the next sections, so you're going to get even more ideas. I suggest you take out a note pad right now so you can jot down anything that may come to mind.

Using the Power of Coupons in Your Marketing Strategy

The first thing you need to do when deciding on whether or not to use coupons in your marketing strategy is to develop a plan to see if they can work for you. Here's what your plan outline should look like:

1. How are you going to use the coupons?

• Do you want to use them to generate leads?

• Give a discount on a big-ticket item so you can sell more of that item?

• Get new customers?

• Get customers who haven't purchased from you in a long time to buy from you?

• Other uses?

2. Who is your target market? Who do you want to reach by adding coupons as part of your marketing strategy?

3. What is your budget? Since this strategy can be used for those with a limited budget, you will want to know exactly how much money you have to spend and in what areas are you going to spend it in? Do you want to spend most of your money on presentation or do you want to spend more of your money on the number of people you can reach with your coupons?

4. How are you going to measure your results? You will need some sort of tracking to see how well this strategy works.

How Do Other Businesses Use Coupon Codes?

I've been in the advertising business for many years and have seen coupons used in thousands of different ways, and in thousands of different businesses. We've all seen the typical X amount of cents off on grocery store coupons. Now even more stores are using coupons that you may be familiar with.

Pharmaceutical stores like Eckerd and Walgreen's now publish an insert in local newspapers that have nothing but coupons for that particular store in them. I know several people who will look for coupons in the paper before doing their shopping for the week. Okay, so you're not a grocery store or big pharmaceutical store, so how can coupons are used in a powerful way for you?

Recently I read James Jones' "12 Little-Known, High Profit, Low Startup, Kick Butt Business Ideas for 2005 and Beyond!" In it he talked about a restaurant he worked at. This restaurant was a small mom and pop type restaurant that did well until a competitor moved in next door. Instead of just going under, this small mom and pop restaurant used the power of coupons to kick their competitors butt. They simply made small buy one lunch get the second lunch free coupons. They distributed these coupons all over their town. The next day, they were totally swamped with business. After counting all the coupons that had been redeemed for that day, they saw that 22% of the coupons they had given away were used.

How many advertising campaigns have you had that gave you a 22% conversion rate? I'd say not many, and probably more like NONE! Let's talk about some online ways coupons have been used.

When I started my web design business in 1998, I had ZERO customers. I had no clue how to get more customers except to offer my services for free and hope for referrals from the people I had done the free web design for. After doing this a couple of times, I saw that I would never make it if I didn't do something different. I started thinking about how to advertise my business. I knew there was a lot of competition out there for web design services, and I somehow had to stick out.

I started by placing classified ads in e-zines. My ad was offering a 50% discount on all web design services. At that time, web design services where sky high and we were in the age of the "Dot Com Boom". When people started seeing these ads, I was flooded with business. I built sites for these people and also added them to my mailing list. When business was slow I'd email my list and offer some type of service such as a "website make over service" or tell them about a new technology they could implement on their site, and again give them a discount. Not like the 50% discount they got at first but more like a 20% discount, and this tactic ALWAYS brought in more business.

I've also offered coupons online for other things such as advertising services, consulting services, tangible products, eBooks, software, and the list goes on. Each and every time I offer a coupon I am not disappointed. People LOVE to save money. How many times have you bought something you really didn't need or want just because it was on sale? As you can see, there are so many ways you can use coupons in your business!

CHAPTER 2- THE EMPATHETIC MARKETING STRATEGY THAT WOWS CUSTOMERS

Discount coupon codes are often given away for free by several companies. Both the online and physical stores give out these coupons which offer several opportunities for the consumers. Would you not be happy to receive discount coupons yourself? For sure you would be!

A Look Back at the Discount Coupon Codes History

The idea about the coupons was openly used by the public back in the year 1902. This was the time when the American manufacturers and merchants started encouraging the consumers to purchase their products up for sale. To trace its history back, it had been the breakfast cereals which initially made use of the discount coupon codes. For these American merchants to gain profit and for their products to become well-known as well, they designated discount coupons as a form of incentive to their prospect buyers. Of course, since most homes can't get rid of taking cereals for their breakfast, they eventually got enticed to purchase the offered product.

Because of the said action, more than seven hundred companies or corporations these days are giving out discount coupons to all and sundry. Surveys prove that some eight billion dollars are generated in the transaction of giving away discount coupons in the entire United States alone. How much more if the total gross profit raised by these discount coupons would be computed for all the countries around the globe?

Today's Concept of the Discount Coupon Codes

The coupon codes that are referred to as of today bear only a few points of difference from those of the discount coupons of the yesteryears. The principle that lies behind the concept of the coupons of today and yesterday still stays the same. Perhaps the most standout characteristic of the discount coupons nowadays lies in the manner of how they are disseminated. Some ten years previously, ecommerce was not yet a strategy that was known to the people. But with the fast pace of today's technological evolutions, business transactions are commonly done through ecommerce now. The world of business largely relies on the use of electronic processing.

The Nature of Coupon Codes

Coupon codes are those that are made available online. Other terms that are used to refer to these are shopping codes, promotional or promotion codes, voucher codes, source codes, discount codes, and promo codes. Besides the discounts from the total selling price that may be availed of by using the regular coupon codes, the coupon codes or those that are rendered via the Internet likewise provides the access to the user to enjoy reduced or free costs for the shipping of the items that have been purchased online, some appropriated percentage price cut, and other worthy offers which may be provided by certain retailers.

Unlike those regular discount coupons that the physical stores furnish you with which may often get lost, the discount coupon codes over the Internet are fraud-protected. Meaning, only the person who owns them can make use of those. There is a kind of registry system that records the number of times the code was or is utilized.

Don't be confused. The general idea here is that the discount coupon codes, those that are bestowed online, work like those paper coupons that you get from the grocery stores. They provide you with huge discounts but in a more technologically savvy way.

What are Target Coupon Codes?

Target is best known for its economical offerings. If you are a smart shopper, however, you will realize that you can still save more money through target coupon codes. What exactly are target coupon codes?

Well, you do know what a discount coupon is, right? It's something that you use in order to reduce the cost of your purchases. Coupon codes serve the same purpose. Instead of a piece of paper, however, what you get is a combination of numbers and letters.

Where does one find coupon codes? Well, most people prefer to go to coupon sites. These sites are popular today because they often contain different types of coupon codes for all your needs.

Pay Less When Shopping

With these sites, you don't have to wait for the latest issue of your trade magazine in order to get your hands on some coupons to reduce your expenses.

These sites, however, may contain only the "generic" coupon codes, or the ones that offer low discounts. It is a rare occasion when one can find a high-end coupon code through a coupon site.

And advantage of going to coupon sites is that these sites often allow you to "save" coupons. This means you won't have to use the code right away in order to avail of a discount. You will be able to save coupons for when you really need them. After all, if you base your purchases around what coupons you have, you might end up buying a lot of unnecessary things.

Most high-end or "special" coupons are distributed to loyal customers through e-mail. If you ever shop at Target.com, you might want to subscribe to one form of newsletter or e-mail alert. This is how most people get their special promotional e-mails with coupon codes.

There is also the option of joining a community and pooling your resources to get some target coupon codes. Yes, this is just paraphrasing the sentence: "you should also consider begging for some coupon codes from other people."

Actually, there are certain consumer groups and communities you can join in order to obtain some coupon codes. In these communities, you are expected to give just as much as you are willing to take. If, for example, you have coupons that you will not be using, you might want to distribute these to other members in exchange for some of the target codes you need.

Are target coupon codes necessary to avail of promos? The answer is no. There are certain promotional campaigns and discounts that do not need you to have a coupon code in order to take advantage of. These promotions, however, are often open to the general public. This means that you might have to go through some competition in order to save some dough.

Coupon codes mainly work for online stores. However, there are also certain target coupon codes, which you may print out and present to the cashier when making a purchase at Target. This means you will be able to avail of the savings offered by these codes even if you don't do much online shopping.

The bottom line is that if you want to obtain target coupon codes, you ought to look for them. Unlike your typical coupons, which you luckily get with a magazine or a newspaper, coupon codes need to be sought.

CHAPTER 3- WHERE TO FIND GREAT COUPON DEALS

Using coupons has always been a great way to save money on the things that you buy regularly, and avid coupon fans will be happy to attest to that. Many people believe, however, that taking the time to find the right coupons is too difficult to make it worth their trouble. This really doesn't have to be the case, however, and the money you save using coupons is well worth finding out how to find the best coupon deals in the easiest way possible.

Online coupons have given a whole new meaning to saving money, and many people are beginning to realize just how easy it is to find them and use them. One way to find online coupons is to simply use an Internet search engine and search for online coupons for the merchandise that you are considering buying. Another way is to use some or all of the many online coupon web sites that are available. Online coupon web sites focus almost exclusively on giving consumers information on what online coupons are available at any given time, and how and where consumers can use them to save money. One of the best ways that online coupon web sites help consumers is by listing "coupon codes" for various online stores. Coupon codes are coupons that are basically all electronic – you simply enter these codes into a special box when you are purchasing something from on online store and the savings are deducted from the price before you finalize your purchase. Online coupon web sites will list the codes that are still valid, and let you know where they can be used. These web sites will almost always update their findings daily, so you can always be aware of what savings are offered at what stores every day. Though you may be able to get these coupon codes through the actual store's web site or through advertisements, it can save you a lot of time to be able to view all the codes at once on one web site.

Finding coupon deals is no problem once you put just a little bit of initial time and research into it. One of the first things that you want to do is go to your favorite search engine and enter such terms as "online coupons", "coupon codes", or perhaps "Internet coupons". The search engine will most likely bring up a large list of web sites that offer online coupons and online coupon codes. Check through a number of the sites and decide which ones have what you are looking for. Once you've narrowed it down to your favorite online coupon web sites, the next step is to put these on your browser's "favorites" list. If any of the online coupon web sites require registration, then do that also. Although there may be online coupon web sites that charge a fee to use them, there are plenty of good online coupon web sites that don't – and the latter are the ones that you want to use. Each day (or every other day if you like), take a little time to log on to the Internet and check your list of online coupon web sites. Look for the latest online coupons codes for the online stores that you frequent regularly and also

Pay Less When Shopping

look for the latest printable coupons that you can use at the local stores that you go to.

For the online coupon codes, you can either write down the codes, how long they are good for and which stores you are going to use them at, or you could possibly keep a list in your own database or spreadsheet. It all depends on how Internet savvy you are or want to be! When it is time to do your online shopping, check your coupon codes, find the ones that you are going to use, and start saving money!

Once you get into the habit of you using online coupons and online coupon codes, especially through online coupon web sites, you'll see the savings that you are realizing almost immediately. In this day and age when the price of just about everything is at an all-time high, using online coupons and online coupon codes makes a great deal of sense. They can help you maintain the lifestyle you are accustomed to without having to stretch your already strained budget even further. Using online coupons to help save money on your regular purchases is a win-win situation all around.

With online coupons and online coupon codes, you can save money on basically any type of purchase. Groceries, appliances, pet products, automobile accessories, hotels, travel fares, restaurant meals – savings can be realized with all of these by using online coupons or online coupon codes. For most of the things that you purchase, there is simply no reason not to use online coupons.

CHAPTER 4- WHY SHIFT TO ONLINE SHOPPING?

Online shopping is a phenomenon that has changed the way we shop for the things we use and need in our day to day lives. An informal survey of web users who frequent an Internet bulletin board that is geared to online shopping reveals that over 90 percent buy products and services online at least once a month, and many of these people make it a habit to shop online several times a week. What is it about this practice that makes them keep going back for more?

If you are one of those people who have yet to shop online, or if you have perhaps completed only one or two transactions online, you don't know what you are missing! Not only have you not experienced the fun of hunting down a good online deal, but you haven't had the satisfaction of saving a bundle of cash on the things you would be buying anyway, online or in a brick and mortar store. Everything that you buy offline can more than likely be found online - from groceries to prescription drugs.

"Sure," you may be thinking. "Online shopping is probably a good thing for people who live miles away from a store. It would almost be a necessity for them in order to have a good selection. But I have all sorts of stores really close to my home. It's more convenient for me to shop the way I always have."

That depends entirely on how you define convenience. Is this really easy?

You get into your car and drive to the store of your choice, then drive around the parking lot a few times looking for a parking space.

 Entering the store, you walk the aisles looking for the things on your list, only to find that they are out of the two most important things you need.

You go back out to your car and drive to your second choice store.

Finally locating the items you need, you stand in an extremely long check-out line behind a woman with a set of 2 year old twins who are screaming for candy.

The cashier is cranky, and acts as if she would rather be doing anything other than her job.

You start back out to your car with your packages, and discover that it is pouring rain. You have no umbrella, and your car is parked way in the back of the lot - the only empty space you could find.

You brave the elements, and make a run for your car, only dropping your packages once. Dripping wet, you turn on the ignition and head for home. It's late afternoon, and the traffic is horrendous. As you inch along, you hear a suspicious little tap-tap-tap on your windshield. A closer look and you groan aloud. The rain has turned into ice.

Meanwhile, your next door neighbor has decided that she is in need of a few health and beauty products. She sits down at her computer in the comfort of her nice, cozy den. A few clicks of her mouse, and her web browser has taken her to an online drugstore that actually offers more of a product variety than the local drugstore that is only a mile from her house. She smiles when she discovers that several of the items on her list are on sale.

As she reaches the screen where she is to finalize her order, she remembers an email she received from this website yesterday. It contained a coupon code that will give her free shipping when she purchases a certain dollar amount. Scanning her order, she sees that she needs to spend $1 more to take advantage of this code. Another few clicks and she added a toothbrush to her virtual shopping cart.

As she clicks the "Place Order Now" icon button, she smiles. That one little code has saved her $8.00! Hearing a sound from outside, she rises and steps over to the window. Pulling back the curtain, she looks outside. It has begun to sleet!

She smiles again as she thinks how nice it is not to have to brave the cold and instead be able to shop from home and have the order delivered right to her front door.

Pay Less When Shopping

Which scenario would you rather find yourself in? The answer should be obvious. Internet shopping can be a much easier alternative for you, especially if you -

- Work long or odd hours and have trouble finding the time to shop after work
- Lack reliable transportation
- Have small children that are difficult to handle on a shopping trip
- Have any sort of physical disability which limits your mobility
- Are looking for items not readily available in your area, such as ethnic foods, classic fragrances, or large shoe and clothing sizes.

Save Time by Buying Online

Shopping online can save you more time than you could imagine. As is illustrated in the scenario above, it is much less of a hassle to make purchases from home, from your office, or anywhere you happen to find a computer than it is to physically shop at the mall or the grocery store. Plus, if you want to shop at 2 AM while wearing your pajamas, you can do that, too!

Online shopping is a lifesaver for Christmas shopping. While everyone else is fighting the crowds, you are greeting the UPS or FedEx driver as your boxes are delivered. You can easily purchase items for gifts without others knowing what you're buying, which comes in very handy when you need to buy gifts for people who live in your home with you. Or maybe you are in need of something that you would rather not have other people know that you use. Online shopping can save you the embarrassment of having nosy strangers or even family members observe your buying habits.

Comparison shopping is a breeze on the Internet. Instead of having to make phone call after phone call, or walk/drive from store to store in search of a product you need, you can do a search on

Google or another search engine in order to locate the best price for an item. Once you locate what you're looking for at a price you want to pay, you are ready to order!

Now, imagine how much more difficult this would have been if you were doing it all the old fashioned way. Let's say you had to visit 10 web sites in order to find the exact product you wanted at a reasonable price. Transpose this shopping equation to real life. By the time you got done with searching 10 brick and mortar stores, you'd be exhausted, and you might even cut your search short and buy the product at a higher price than you had expected to pay in order to finish your shopping and go home! With online shopping, you won't have this problem.

"But I need an item TODAY," you might say. "I don't want to have to wait until an online store can ship my purchase to me!" If you are in a hurry for an item, you can sometimes order it online and then pick it up at the store, as long as there is a store available in your area. Office supply stores and department stores with a web presence usually offer this feature to their online customers. It can be a real time saver as all you need to do is go to the Customer Service desk to pick up your order.

You can also choose to pay an extra shipping fee when ordering online in order to have your items sent to you sooner, even overnight, but the cost of this could very well negate any savings you may have realized by using a coupon code.

Here is where you have to sit down and decide what your priorities are. Is the hassle of navigating your way through crowded stores and having to search for the items you want to buy, plus the chore of standing in long checkout lines to pay for the items better than the convenience of ordering the items online and having to wait a few days before you receive your order?

Pay Less When Shopping

For most people, the convenience of online shopping far outweighs the minor inconvenience of not being able to take possession of their purchase immediately. Try both scenarios, and then make your decision. I'll bet you choose online shopping!

This is probably why online shopping has become one of the most popular ways to shop. You have so many choices, and can custom tailor your shopping habits to suit yourself.

Online Shopping and Coupon Codes

Be aware that some coupon codes expire very quickly, while others can be valid for quite some time. When you enter the code, whatever discount it represents is immediately taken off of the total of your order. It's a good idea to check your total on the checkout page once you refresh it to make sure the code went through.

Occasionally, coupon codes are removed without notice by the retailer. And, sometimes a coupon code is so popular that the web site where you use it is jammed with customers! If this happens, you might have to try your code more than one time to get it to go through. If you've done this, and your coupon code still does not work, a call to the Customer Service department of the retailer might be in order. Usually, the telephone number to call if you have any questions is listed somewhere on the web site.

Some web sites also have live help where you can actually chat with a customer representative in an instant-message type setting. They are quick to answer any questions you might have, as they realize that a happy customer is usually a repeat customer. Or, look for the store's email address. This is just one of the many neat things about shopping on the Internet - most of the time, help is but a mouse click away.

Make sure you understand the terms of the coupon code. If it states that you must spend $25 to get that 10% off, don't think you can squeak by with spending $24.98! You have to spend the stated amount down to the last cent. Luckily, most online stores will have items for sale that are quite cheap - in the case of Amazon.com. 5 cents or even less! This makes it easy to add another item to your shopping cart to bring up your total.

Also, don't confuse coupon codes with rebates! Unlike a manufacturer's mail in rebate, an online coupon code saves you money the instant you use it.

The Different Types of Coupon Codes

Coupon codes are called promotional codes by some online retailers. Don't let this confuse you - they are the same thing, really. Most of the time, the online codes are a series of numbers, numbers and letters mixed, or a short word that relates to the type of retailer, usually in all capital letters. For example, a PetSmart code could look like this -

MEOW838

Another type of code is a clickable link that leads you to a page where a number/letter code will be displayed for you to enter when you check out. These codes are often included in email newsletters that online retailers send to customers who have signed up for them.

If you think about it, you'll realize that an online coupon is merely a more modern version of the coupons shoppers have been clipping from the Sunday newspaper inserts for many years. And, like those paper coupons, online coupons can be found for almost any

Pay Less When Shopping

product that is sold on the Internet. You should be able to find coupon codes for the following -

- Clothing for Men, Women and Children
- Auto accessories
- Health and Beauty Ads
- Pet Food and Accessories
- Magazines and Books
- Computers and computer accessories
- Gifts and Flowers
- Electronics
- Furniture
- Food
- Sporting Goods
- Shoes
- Jewelry
- Art and Photography
- Office Supplies
- Online Services
- Music CDs, Movie DVDs, Video Games'
- Kitchen accessories, including cookware
- Gardening and Outdoor supplies
- Toys and Games
- Cigarettes and Cigars
- Airline Tickets
- Concert and Event Tickets
- Rental Cars
- Hotel Accommodations
- Restaurants

In short, anything that is sold on the Internet by a retailer or company, large or small, can have a coupon code associated with it. You will sometimes see multiple codes, and in this case, you should stop and figure out which one would give you the best value. When you are just starting out using coupons online to save money, this all might seem a little confusing. But, after you've completed a transaction or two, you will catch on like an old pro.

For example, let's say that you want to do some shopping at The Body Shop online. Your first step is to visit a website devoted to coupon codes in order to see if there are any current ones for this retailer. You spy not just one, but several codes. There is one that offers you free shipping on your order another which gives you 10% off of the total amount you spend, and another that is for $10 off when you spend $25. How will you know which one to use?

Depending on how much you are planning to spend, it's a tossup between the $10 off and the 10% off. On some web sites, you can use more than one coupon code, which is called stacking. This is a very popular method for maximum savings, and a perfectly legitimate option. You won't know if a retailer will allow the use of multiple codes until you actually type them into the space on the order blank and update the page to see if they went through. If they did, you will notice that your total amount due has been reduced. If they didn't you will see a brief message, sometimes in red text that explains why you were not given the discount. It's well worth your time to try multiple coupon codes each time you shop online!

The codes themselves are somewhat predictable. Generally, they are like the ones in the example above - a percentage or a flat amount off of your total bill, or free shipping. There have also been instances, usually seasonal, where the addition of a special coupon code will yield a free gift.

CHAPTER 5- WHICH STORES ARE KNOWN TO OFFER COUPON CODES?

EBay

Online shopping has never been more rewarding and convenient than it is today. Every year an increasing number of people surf the Internet to search for and purchase items from online stores like the popular auction site eBay.com. As a result, websites continuously create ways to increase both their profitability and their shoppers' satisfaction.

Coupon codes are among the promotional strategies ecommerce sites use. eBay.com, for example offers free eBay coupon codes, which can be used by online shoppers to get discounts on items they purchase at eBay.com. They are similar to traditional discount coupons used by retail stores to encourage more shoppers to buy at their stores.

EBay coupon codes are widely available online but are fully utilized. These free eBay coupon codes when used to purchase high priced items auctioned at the site translate to huge savings. A mere 5% discount could be equal to hundreds or even thousands of dollars when the item purchased is unique and a valuable one.

EBay usually send free eBay coupon codes to their members through email. If you receive one of them, take advantage of these codes or else you lose the opportunity to avail of their special discounts and privileges. Since these free eBay coupon codes are sent to you, you may have to validate your identity when purchasing an item at eBay and upon using the electronic discount code. You may not be able to give the code to another person. However, if it's not indicted in the email that you may not be able to share your free eBay coupon code, it is safe to assume that you can give it to someone else. EBay discount codes that can be shared to others are often found at eBay's chat forums. If you intend to find a free eBay coupon code and give it to a friend, then this is the best place to search for them.

Electronic eBay codes like other coupon codes have expiration dates. They are valid only within a certain period of time so it is important that you use them as soon as you get them.

Once you find a free eBay coupon code, you can use it at once. All you have to do is to purchase the item you want the usual way. At the billing page, you will find a space where you would have to enter the eBay coupon code. After you enter the code, eBay will validate it and the discount will automatically be reduced from the total amount of the item purchased.

Discounts won't be deducted from the seller's income; in fact, that person won't be able to know that you purchased the item at a discounted price using a free eBay coupon code. So if it's your turn to sell an item at eBay, don't fret, you income is all yours while your buyer buys the item you're selling at a much favorable price.

Find as much free eBay coupon codes as you can to increase your chances of getting great discounts. In order to increase your savings, find free eBay coupon codes that match high priced items. Regularly check eBay and sites offering listings of electronic coupon codes so you won't miss a chance to avail of greater deals at eBay.

Old Navy

Old Navy prides itself in being able to serve fashion-conscious and price-conscious individuals. They offer high-end clothing at affordable prices for the whole family. However, did you know that you could make purchases at this shop even more affordable simply by getting Old Navy coupon codes online?

Yes, it's true- you can save so much more by making use of coupon codes whenever you shop. There are two types of coupon codes according to their usage:

A) Online – most coupon codes today come under this category. This type of coupon code may only be used when buying at the online Old Navy shop. With this type of coupon code, you may be able to reduce the cost of your online purchases, which could be pretty heavy, considering the delivery fees.

B) Offline/Online – there are also certain coupon codes which may be utilized both off and on the Internet. These coupons may often be found on websites coupled with printable barcodes. There are also certain coupons found on magazines, which contain codes that can be entered on Internet shopping sites.

So you can see, you have different options open to you if you want to save some cash on your purchases. This means you have the power to choose how the coupon codes should be utilized. You control your purchases.

Saving cash on Old Navy coupon codes, however, may be a bit disorienting. Not many people realize this, but coupon codes are actually advertising tools. This means a coupon code is used to convince you to spend money.

The only way you can keep an eye on the "saving money" objective is if you do not base your purchases on what sort of coupon is available. It should be the other way around- you need to apply the proper coupons to your purchases. Doing so will enable you to maximize savings without falling into the marketing trap.

Another way that you can save money in using coupons is by making sure that you pick the right coupon for the right transaction. That is, you need to learn how to maximize the amount you save every time you make a purchase. Learn to compute and then to compare the value of coupons when you consider the total cost of your purchases. Learn to think in terms of percentages, not dollars.

You should make sure not to waste coupon codes. A good idea is to try and avoid impulse shopping. Before you shop, you should have a rough idea about what sort of purchases you will be making. This allows you to plan your purchases properly and actually find corresponding coupons.

Pay Less When Shopping

There are a number of Old Navy items that are only available online. If you are planning to buy these items, then you might want to make sure that you have the right coupon codes. Looking for coupon codes for these items shouldn't be a hard task, seeing as how you will be searching for something very specific.

These are just some of the ways that you can save money using Old Navy coupon codes. You should also try to find out if there are any promos that you can avail of together with the coupon codes for even bigger savings. After all, you do want to save all the money that you can.

Walmart

Walmart is the world's largest public corporation by revenue. However, this is not because they sell expensive items. In fact, many people know Walmart because of its discounted items. Did you know that you can use Walmart coupon codes and reduce your shopping costs even more?

As you may realize, online shopping may be more convenient, but it also costs more. This is primarily because of the shipping fees involved. However, with coupon codes, you can make your shopping experience more convenient and less expensive.

How do you obtain such codes? Well, you need to look for them or you need to earn them. If you want to look for coupon codes, you should check out various coupon sites. Believe it or not, there are actually sites where you can search for all the coupons you want. These sites are often paid by companies like Walmart to distribute coupons (which are actually advertising tools) to the general public.

When you look for codes in coupon sites you will be getting some pretty great opportunities to save cash. However, if you want to have truly spectacular offers, you might want to check out other sources.

One of the best sources of coupon codes would be from the shopping site itself. Regular visitors to the site, when they give their email address, may be given various alerts regarding special offers and promos. E-mails are sent to them, which may include a coupon code or two.

What makes this type of coupon code distinctive from something that you can get from coupon sites is that a coupon received through email promos is usually good for more than a single use. This means you can have more and more savings!

It has also been observed by some people that coupon codes received through promotional e-mail often contain a much higher discount rate than your typical coupons. This is primarily because discount coupons distributed to regular customers are designed to make them feel rewarded and to encourage them to continue their patronage. This is also done in order to avoid coupon wastage.

Why should you not waste coupons? Well, you should realize that coupons equal money. These codes have value. They can be accounted for. This means not using them or allowing them to expire without extracting their value would be tantamount to throwing away your money.

How do you extract the best value form your codes? Well, the first thing you should do is budget your cash properly. If you plan on shopping at Walmart or in its website, you should first think about the things that you plan to buy. When you have a list of the various items that you need, you should then try to find the coupons for them. Most people do this the other way around: they first get the coupons and then modify their purchases to suit the coupons. This might be dangerous for a person working with a tight budget.

Never forget that a coupon code is distributed as part of an advertising campaign. If you forget this fact, you might end up spending too much of your cash instead of saving it. Shopping with Walmart coupon codes requires you to be smart and always keep in mind that there are plenty of opportunities out there to save your cash.

Macy's

Macy's is one of the biggest department store chains in the United States. However, their different flagship and suburban stores are only a part of Macy's. Today, a lot of people are discovering the convenience of shopping online at Macy's site. And with this convenience comes another development in the form of Macy's coupon codes.

Macy's coupon codes allow a person to shop at the Macy's online store for reduced prices. Let's face it: no one has unlimited funding and we all want to save our money whenever we can. Macy's coupon codes allow us to accomplish precisely this, if we use the codes right.

If you do not know how to use the codes properly, you might end up wasting money instead of saving some. Here are different sources you can use in order to get some coupon codes:

1) E-mail alerts – if you shop frequently at Macy's you might have encountered a prompt or two requesting that you input your e-mail address in order to receive alerts. This is pretty much like the mailing list of a department store. E-mails will be sent to you every time there's a special offer or promo at Macy's. This will let you

know when there's an opportunity for savings that you might want to take advantage of.

E-mail alerts, as many people will tell you, also contain the best types of coupon codes. This is frequently because the codes contained in email alerts are made specifically for you. They are also good for multiple, albeit limited uses. Coupons contained in these alerts also have the biggest discount rates.

2) Coupon sites – there are a lot of websites dedicated solely to the distribution of coupon codes today. Membership in these sites may not be required to get coupons. However, the member ship is essential if you want to make your coupon-hunting experience a lot easier.

A typical browser may be able to locate your typical coupons in sites like these. That is, you will be able to find some codes that would help you save cash, but don't expect anything spectacular.

Besides these two sources, you should realize that you have millions of people at your fingertip through the Internet. Surely, with a resource as big as this, you can network and find the codes that you want. Once you get the codes, however, what are you going to do with them? Here are a few tips to help you make sure that you extract the best value from your coupons:

A) Plan what you buy – a common reason for overspending is impulse buying. When you first enter any department store, you will be assaulted by a variety of advertising tactics. All these advertising efforts are directed at one goal: getting you to spend your cash. This is true even for online shops. In order to protect yourself from overspending, you need to make sure that you have a clear budget to follow. Planning also helps you make sure that you have all the right coupons when you shop.

B) Choose the right coupons – if you have more than one coupon you can use, try and make sure that you pick the right ones to use in shopping. You need to carefully compare the potential savings offered by each coupon and choose the coupon that offers the biggest discount for you.

Toys R Us

Toys R Us is the second biggest toy store chain in the United States. People all over the world know about Toys R Us. This may be partly because the company holds a base of operations that reaches out throughout the planet. This base of operations is otherwise known as the Internet. Because of the popularity of online shopping today, many people are looking for various types of Toys R Us coupon codes, which can help them, save on their purchases.

Coupon codes are sequences of numbers that activate a discount or a special promo when entered in the checkout area of a shopping site. There are also certain codes that are attached to a prearranged electronic "shopping cart". There are a variety of advantages that you can get from coupon codes. Here are some of them:

1) Savings – the first thing that attracts people to the use of coupon codes is the fact that they represent savings. As you may undoubtedly realize, buying toys can be very taxing to the pocket (no pun intended). They are considered in the category of wants and not needs.

Still, people want to save cash wherever they can and they use coupons to avail of discounts and promos just to make sure that they get the biggest value from their hard-earned money. After all, do not those crisp green bills and that two-digit number represent hour of your time, trickles of your sweat?

This is more evident in a world where convenience is a ready commodity and where people would rather sit and watch TV than get lost in aisles of smiling clowns, dolls and action figures. The shipping and delivery costs aren't getting any lower. If you want to have the convenience you have to pay the price. But if you have the right coupon code, you might just have the convenience for free, its cost absorbed by the lower price of the item.

2) Convenience – coupon codes attached to prearranged shopping carts are quite common. In a world where microwave dinners and instant "everything" prevails, this should not be surprising. With a coupon code like this, you won't even have to go through the trouble of picking the right toy for your kid. All you have to do is swipe the code, pay the merchandise and voila! You are done shopping.

This convenience is quite important, considering the fact that this is what most people are after when they go to an online store.

3) Special offers – there are certain coupon codes that allow a person to obtain items only available to regular customers. These coupons are highly valued and are distributed most often by email to regular customers who shop frequently on the Toys R Us site. By availing of these coupon codes, you are given the opportunity not just to collect toys, but memories.

Getting Toys R Us coupon codes is certainly the smart way to go. Looking at all the benefits, you might want to jump right away and start hunting for the codes you need to make your toy shopping easier. However, you should also realize that coupons are advertising tools. Try to make sure that you stick to the budget you planned instead of using the budget indicated by the coupon codes; you might end up spending more than you intended to.

Chapter 6- Does Using Coupons Really Guarantee Savings?

The popularity of online coupon codes has really begun to catch on, and every day, more and more people are realizing that they can save quite a bit on the things they need when they take advantage of these discounts. With a little planning, you can too!

It helps to have some patience, especially if you are just starting out. Sometimes, you will not be able to find a coupon code for the online store where you want to shop. Though there are usually lots of valid coupon codes circulating around the Web, every store will not always have one listed. If that is the case, you can choose to wait and make your purchase when a code becomes available, or perhaps choose a different store that does have a code that will allow you to save some money.

Another more indirect way that online coupon codes can save you money is the savings you will realize at the gas pump and on your car maintenance. Gasoline prices are high and there seems to be no relief in sight any time soon. When you shop online, you don't have to drive to the store, using up expensive gasoline and putting more miles on your car. On average, depending on the kind of car you drive, it costs anywhere from 35 to 40 cents for each mile you drive – not including the gas! So, it's easy to see how shopping online can help you save a nice chunk of change in a year's time.

We spoke of saving time in the paragraphs above, but the subject is well worth mentioning again. Few people put a price on their time, but you should. Your time is very valuable! Every minute of time that you save by shopping online instead of having to get the car out and drive to the store is a minute that you can put toward making your life more productive. Next time you go to the mall, do a little experiment. Keep track of how much time it takes you to fight the traffic in order to drive there, find the items you are looking for, pay for them, and drive home again. You will be shocked! Now, see how that time can add up over the course of a year? Remember – time is money!

Some people have tried online shopping, and are quite vocal about the cost of shipping. Obviously, they did not pursue the fun of using coupon codes, nor did they even try online shopping more than a time or two. If they had, they would have seen that not only do online coupon codes for free shipping pop up for most retail stores on the web with regularity, but most stores will offer free shipping even without a coupon code if you spend a set amount, usually $30 or so. So, this argument is a moot point. Online shopping with coupon codes can and does save savvy shoppers quite a bit of money!

One thing you need to be aware of is that if you have an actual brick and mortar store in your area that also has an online presence, you will pay sales tax on your purchases from the web. This adds a small amount to your total invoice amount. For example, if you have a Best Buy in your city, and you order an iPod from BestBuy.com, you'll be charged sales tax. Or, if you purchase a pair of jeans from Old Navy.com, and there is no Old Navy store in your city, you will not have to pay sales tax.

Should You Really Use Online Coupons?

Have you ever trudged through the mall, going into store after store looking for just the right birthday gift for your best friend? Or, have you ever tried to find an article of clothing in a particular color shade, only to be told over and over, "Sorry, we don't have that in stock."? How about a popular book, DVD movie or music CD that you just have to have, but to your dismay, every store you check has sold out of the title?

Maybe you are buying a wedding gift for your cousin. She wants a certain silverware pattern, and so far you've had no luck in finding it. In desperation, you haul out the Yellow Pages and call each store listed that you think might have the elusive pattern, but again, you are out of luck. Or maybe your favorite curling iron or electric razor has stopped working. You go back to the store where you purchased it, only to find that they no longer sell that particular brand.

Were you one of the many people who were standing in line this past holiday season outside of an electronics superstore at the crack of dawn, after camping out on the sidewalk all night? You were hoping and praying that when the doors opened, you would be one of the select few who were able to purchase one of the latest and greatest video game systems that the store had received a shipment of only 10 units the day before.

Perhaps you and a group of your friends gathered outside the Ticketmaster box office early in the evening and stood in line until they opened at midnight in order to grab concert tickets for your favorite music act before they were all sold out.

Or, maybe you need airline tickets, but you only want to spend a certain amount. You know you are supposed to be able to get a good deal if you purchase your tickets two weeks in advance, but when you call the airlines, they quote you an outrageous price that's nothing like the price you expected to pay.

In all of these scenarios, shopping online with a valid coupon code could save you time, trouble, and money. You could spend a pleasant hour browsing stores on the web for a gift that would thrill your best friend, and if you used a coupon code when paying for it, you could either pocket the difference, or maybe put it toward a little bit nicer gift than you had originally planned to give.

That shirt you are looking for in just the right shade of red can be easily found on the Internet. There are hundreds of clothing web sites. Most have photos of the items they sell, color charts, and size charts. Some even have virtual models that you can customize with your own measurements, and then use to "try on" the clothes. You would more than likely have no trouble at all finding exactly what you are looking for, pay a bargain price with the help of a coupon code, and enjoy the process to boot.

Popular DVDs and music CDs and best-seller books can sell out online as well as in a brick and mortar store. But, many places online that sell these items will allow you to preorder them well before the date they are due to be released. The price is almost always better in an online store. Why? Because of the coupon code that is generally issued in anticipation of the rush of people who want to preorder. You get an excellent price and sometimes free shipping when the item is sent to you.

Items that seem almost impossible to find or that may have been discontinued are often quite easy to find on the web. It's much easier to use a search engine to track down that elusive silverware pattern than it is to go from store to store or spend half the day on the phone looking for it. There are retail web sites specializing in china and silverware which have hundreds and hundreds of patterns for you to choose from. Most of these stores offer to do whatever they can to help you locate exactly the pattern you seek. And, you'd be surprised at just how often this type of store offers a coupon code for its customers.

Discontinued or hard to find small electrical appliances such as curling irons and razors can be located on the web by using a special search engine that finds such items easily, often still in the original packaging, A search on a comparison shopping web site such as BizRate.com or Pricegrabber.com will bring back a list of stores which sell the item you want, plus a list of the prices ranging from low to high. Add a coupon code to one of the low prices, and you're all set for several more years with your favorite small appliance that you thought you'd never see again.

As for that concert ticket, or even a movie ticket for the latest box office hit, both can be easily booked online at Ticketmaster.com for concert tickets, and Fandango.com for movie tickets. There are even coupon codes available online for these establishments!

Ticketmaster has had codes available that for example will give you a $98 ticket to a musical for $60, half off on certain movie tickets, and 20% off on Ringling Brothers Circus tickets.

Fandango's codes have ranged from Buy one; get one free to a $1 movie ticket. This is the easiest and best way to go to a concert or movie. No hassle, no stress. Order online, get a discount by using a coupon code, and pick your tickets up at the theater the day or evening of the show. What could be easier?

Online retailers are pretty savvy folks themselves. When you shop online at a web site for the first time, you are usually invited to register. Of course, you can decline, as you can still do business with the merchant even without giving him your email address and other pertinent info, but some information is needed so your order can be tracked, if necessary. Registration does make it easier when you go back to shop with a merchant for the second time. All you need to do is sign in with your email and password, and your information will be placed onto the order form for you.

Drugstore.com is a retailer that takes this a step further. When you buy items from their web site such as health and beauty aids or vitamins, they calculate the time it should take you to use them up. After this time has passed, then send you an email with a gentle reminder that it's time to order again! Very convenient... and very smart of Drugstore.com!

This is one way a website lures you back for that next purchase. Another way they can get your attention is to send well-timed emails to you that outline any sales they may be having. Usually, a coupon code or two will be included in this email, for you are now considered to be a "preferred customer". These stores want your business!

Online coupon codes can turn up in the most surprising places. You would not think that a high end store would offer much in the way of coupon codes or discounts, but they most certainly do, and good ones, too. This is a fantastic way to own luxury items that you may not be able to afford otherwise. It is not an unusual occurrence to buy a beautiful sweater that retails for hundreds of dollars for just a fraction of that price when you combine a sale with a coupon code.

Another reason why you should use online coupon codes is to be able to take advantage of the vast assortment of goods and services available on the Internet at a bargain price. If you live in a part of the country that does not have certain national chain stores, you can still shop at any of them from the comfort of your home. Or, if you live far from a big city and do not have many stores to choose from when you get ready to shop for clothing, items for your home, or anything else, you can turn to the Internet to find what you are looking for. Combine a world of choices with a coupon code that will save you money, and you have got quite a winning combination!

CHAPTER 7- WHAT TO AVOID WHEN USING COUPON CODES

Now that you are all excited about the money you can save using coupon codes, there are a few things you need to know in order to keep yourself safe while shopping online.

• A disturbing trend has come to light on auction sites such as EBay where unsuspecting shoppers are actually buying coupon codes that are supposed to be free! This is not a good idea, and steps as being taken as of this writing to have the offending auctions pulled. Why would you want to pay for something that is meant to be free? The people who are running these auctions are counting on the fact that some shoppers will not realize that these codes are available for free all over the web.

• Stick with stores that you know are legitimate when shopping online with coupon codes. If you run across a web store offering you an incredible coupon code like $75 off when you spend $100 or something equally as absurd, run, don't walk! This web site is more than likely after personal information such as your credit card number, and if you give it out to them, you may find a lot of unauthorized charges on your statement next month. As the old saying goes, if it seems just too good to be true, it probably is.

• When searching for a web site than contains information about online shopping and coupon codes, make sure you are using a site that offers you fresh, up to date codes. It's very discouraging to click through to an expired coupon code thinking you are about to get a good deal, and instead you get nothing. Don't settle for a site that just has a bunch of codes up on a page, either. At the very least, you want links to the online stores where the codes are to be used.

• Choose a coupon code web site that seems friendly. You want to be able to ask questions when you need to, so a web site with a forum where shoppers can congregate and exchange ideas and thoughts about online shopping is ideal, especially for someone new to online shopping. Look for an email address where you can contact the owner of the web page if a forum is not present.

You should be able to view the coupon codes on a web site without having to give out your email address. Now, don't be alarmed when you come across a site that does ask for this information. You don't have to give it out if you don't want to. But usually, the site asks you to register if you want to take part in the forums, or to receive occasional emails about the web site. If a web site is asking for your information seemingly for no reason, back off. They may be simply harvesting email addresses, and if you give yours out, you may well wind up with an email inbox full of spam.

CHAPTER 8- MAXIMIZING COUPON CODES

Now that you have read about how easy it is to save some serious money with online coupon codes, it's time to learn a few tips to help you to make the most of the codes you will be using.

• You're ready to check out and use that great coupon code you found for $10 off when you spend $20, but your items total $19.86. Sure, you could add another item that costs a dollar, but why spend more than you have to? There are very handy little tools on that help you find what online shoppers commonly call "filler items".

- Filler items are things that cost very little, and hence are used to make up those last few cents needed to bring your order total up to a certain amount. It would take you a mighty long time to go through a huge web site like Amazon.com looking for items that cost 10 cents (yes, such items do exist) so Pricetaker's tool is innovative and quite a timesaver, too.

- To use this tool, choose your store from the drop down box, then enter the price range you want to see items from. Try .01 to .05 for starters – you will be surprised how many items come up! Now you can pick out one or more things to bring your order total to the amount needed!

- The web site Couponwinner.com has a nifty little tool called Coupon Scout. It allows you to select a category, choose up to 5 different stores from a long list, then compare the coupon codes they have to offer. It is a quick way to see what's available, especially if you are in a hurry.

- If you want to be a really smart online shopper, and the idea of missing a good deal makes you almost want to cry, choose several of your favorite sites that offer coupon codes. Bookmark them in their own folder so you can refer back to them daily. And, it goes without saying – always search for a valid coupon code before every online purchase!

- Everyone has their favorite "real" stores… those you actually walk into and make a purchase as opposed to buying an item online. One of the best tips I ever received was to always check the online stores for coupon code specials before you shop their brick and mortar counterparts. Often you will find a better deal online than in the actual store, and then you take action and buy the item.

Pay Less When Shopping

- Plan your shopping so that you are able to meet any purchase requirements necessary to use the online code. If you have to spend $50 in order to use the coupon code, look the web site over carefully and make a list of the things you need and could buy in order to bring your total spent up to the amount you need.

- Choose your favorite online stores. They will offer newsletters or special mailings to their customers who have signed up to receive them, and often these will have coupon codes in the form of special discount links that the general public does not see.

- Coupon code web sites will also publish newsletters, and it would be worth your while to subscribe to a few of them as well to keep abreast of any new codes that have been released. These stores and/or web sites won't fill up your inbox, nor will they spam you!

- Generally, you can expect an email from an online store or web site maybe once a week – usually less often – but sometimes, more often. It all depends on how many new coupon codes there are.

- Think of it like this... receiving emails from your favorite online stores can actually save you a lot of time. You won't have to go to the actual website in order to keep up with the latest deals.

- Read. Read magazines. Read newspapers. And, watch commercials! The idea here is to keep up with the latest trends. You need to know how much things cost in order to be able to determine whether or not something is a good buy.

- Paying attention to prices can actually save you money in the long run. A coupon code is not a good deal if you use it to buy something that is a cheap imitation of a quality product.

- Don't snatch up the first bargain you see for a really big ticket item, coupon code or not. Make certain you can't get it for a better price anywhere else. You never know when an even better bargain may be lurking just around the corner!

- Try not to be in a hurry when you shop. This is yet another reason why shopping online is so great! Think about it – Don't you think the stress level is a lot lower for someone who is sitting at home, relaxed at their computer with their feet propped up, surfing the Internet for bargains than it is for the person standing in a store inside a crowded mall trying to catch the eye of a salesperson in order to ask a question?.

Would you like to make money for your child's college education while you are shopping? There are web sites that will give you back a small percentage of the money you use to purchase items. When you buy something, a percentage of what you spend is deposited into your account. It is a painless way to save a little money which can build up over time into a surprisingly large amount!

ABOUT THE AUTHOR

Betty Wright works as a financial consultant to high net-worth families. Over the years, she has built a portfolio of successful businesses that were born from her interactions with her clients and the resulting pieces of business advice

www.ingramcontent.com/pod-product-compliance
Lightning Source LLC
Chambersburg PA
CBHW051251170526
45165CB00004B/1659